Foreword

We often make God complicated and distant. In Growing Up Catholic in Pittsburgh, author Regina Munsch has captured the nearness of God and our Catholic faith through simple illustrations and poetry calling to mind that, if we have eyes to see, God is present right where we live in Pittsburgh — in nature, the work of our hands and in the people.

Sister Annie Bremmer, OSF

I would not have been able to publish this book without the help of some very special people. First and foremost, I would like to thank the Girl Scouts of the USA for giving me the opportunity to complete my Gold Award. Thank you to the Faith Formation catechists and students at Saints John & Paul Parish of Franklin Park, PA for the beautiful artwork that is featured in this book. Much gratitude goes to Sister Annie Bremmer, OSF for being my mentor in this project and providing so much inspiration and support. Special thank you to Jeff Comella Photography for the headshot. Many thanks to Susie and Jay Hernishin of SJH Design for bringing my book and website visions to life. Finally, the biggest thanks go to my parents, Bill and Roslyn, and my older sister, Maria, for their endless support in all facets of my life. Simply said: I could not have done this without you — thank you.

Regina Munsch

*A*llegheny, Monongahela, and Ohio are their names, our beloved rivers are three.

Whenever you see them, remind yourself of the **Holy Trinity.**

Panthers, Pirates,
    Steelers, and Penguins;
our Pittsburgh sports teams
    are plenty!

For our teams to win,
    we must cheer loud—
just as when we pray,
    we make **God proud!**

Our beloved city comes to a point where a fountain sits and flows, the Point State Park Fountain reminds us of ho

od's great love always grows!

The Jack Rabbit,
Racer,
Thunderbolt,
Exterminator,
Phantom's Revenge,
Sky Rocket, and Steel Curtain
are Kennywood's seven roller coaster thrills;

and the Seven Sacraments of Baptism,
Reconciliation,
Holy Eucharist,
Confirmation,
Marriage,
Holy Orders, and Anointing of the Sick
are the best way to be **Godly and fulfilled!**

Pittsburgh loves celebrating birthdays
in December by the Steel Building downtown;
visiting the **Nativity** where Jesus' family prayed
makes it impossible to leave with a frown!

*I*n the winter snow when Lent begins
and on Fridays we go without meat,
churches have fish fries — with pierogi, too —
honoring God with Pittsburgh treats!

The Pope is the head
of the Catholic Church,
he lives in the Holy See;
Our Bishop prays
at St. Paul Cathedral,
leading our **Pittsburgh Diocese!**

Pittsburgh has more than 400 bridges that connect communities each day. Our bridge to the Lord's Heavenly Town is to **join together and pray.**

All around Pittsburgh lie many universities
where you go to learn something new;
God is our teacher at Mass each week
from the instant you enter the pew!

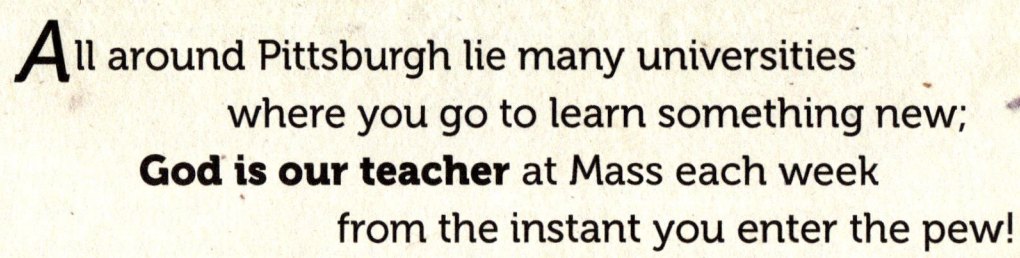

Ride up the Incline to see Mt. Washington's spectacular view, look at God's creations and remember that **He loves you!**

Illustrations By:

Ralph Abdel-Massih	Nolan Hudec	Molly Mooney
Brock Baldwin	Carson Jacobs	Adrianna Najjar
Colin Barrett	Eli Janowiak	John Notaro
Mia Brinkley	Julianna Joyce	Peter Notaro
Max Bywalski	Allison Kapanowski	Allison Phillips
Ben Clawson	Thomas Kapanowski	Juliana Romanelli
Olivia Codol	Leo Laschon	Luca Scolieri
Owen Donley	Alison Lee	Gus Stedeford
Alexander Dorsch	Josie Lesinski	Jackson Talerico
Gabby Frank	Anna Maggi	Rebecca Thompson
Mary Kate Griffin	Shea Mahon	Julianne Weaver
Preston Herzog	Lydia Martorella	Cole Wilson
Madelyn Hudec	Clare Mooney	Grace Zahorchak

www.ingramcontent.com/pod-product-compliance
Lightning Source LLC
Chambersburg PA
CBHW042145290426
44110CB00002B/125